THE NEW
Western Home

THE NEW
Western Home

CHASE REYNOLDS EWALD

PHOTOGRAPHS BY AUDREY HALL

GIBBS SMITH
TO ENRICH AND INSPIRE HUMANKIND
Salt Lake City | Charleston | Santa Fe | Santa Barbara

First Edition
14 13 12 11 10 09   5 4 3 2 1

Published by
Gibbs Smith
P.O. Box 667
Layton, Utah 84041

1.800.835.4993 orders
www.gibbs-smith.com

Designed and produced by Adrienne Pollard
Printed and bound in China
Gibbs Smith books are printed on either recycled, 100% post-
consumer waste, FSC-certified papers or on paper produced
from a 100% certified sustainable forest/controlled wood source.

Library of Congress Cataloging-in-Publication Data

Ewald, Chase Reynolds, 1963-
  New western home / Chase Reynolds Ewald ; photographs by
Audrey Hall. — 1st ed.
      p. cm.
  ISBN-13: 978-1-4236-0255-2
  ISBN-10: 1-4236-0255-2
  1. Interior decoration—West (U.S.) 2. Decoration and ornament,
Rustic—West (U.S.) I. Hall, Audrey. II. Title.
  NK2008.E97 2009
  728.0978—dc22
                        2009000688

acknowledgments

It doesn't take much to put me in a western state of mind. For this lifelong passion I have my parents to thank. They sent me to camp 2,500 miles away at age eleven so that I could wake to the sight of the Tetons every morning, ride western, and learn outdoor skills. Little did they know my Teton Valley Ranch experience would change the course of my life.

I owe a huge debt to Oak Thorne, who gave me my first wrangling job, and to Duane and Sheila Hagen at Hidden Valley Ranch, who hired me sight unseen because my horse was a good hand. Bo Polk and Bob Curtis stepped out on a limb when they backed me in running Breteche Creek Ranch, a nonprofit educational guest ranch in a remote valley with no electricity or phone. All these people taught me about western hospitality, western design, and western can-do; if it weren't for them I wouldn't be doing what I do today.

In the making of this book, many people invited Audrey Hall and me to share their campfire. We extend our heartfelt thanks to John and Kathryn Heminway, Hilary Heminway, David and Alexia Leuschen, Tom and Patty Agnew and the Women of the Wild West, George Wanless and Karen Carson, Chris Ellis, Foster and Lynn Freiss, Pete and Melanie Lovelace, Randy and Diane Ross, Doug Tedrow, and Tom and Nancy McCoy. For sharing their thoughts on design and the changing western landscape, we are deeply grateful to Jonathan Foote, Larry Pearson, Rain Turrell, Lori Ryker, Doug Minarik, Tom Norquist, Dave Strike, Kerry Strike, Wally Reber of the Buffalo Bill Historical Center, Ken Siggins, Jim and Lynda Covert, Rossi Scott, and Scott Boettger of the Wood River Land Trust.

For their gracious hospitality, ongoing support, and enthusiasm, we can never begin to repay Sue Simpson Gallagher, Chuck Neustifter, Dan and Deb Stegelman, Sally Boettger, Kerry Strike, Hannah Ballantyne, Debra Chase, and Todd W. Harris, PhD.

Our meticulous editor, Lisa Anderson, undoubtedly saved us from our mistakes; designer extraordinaire Adrienne Pollard presented our work in the best possible light. Thank you both!

And, finally, for their love, support, and patience in our own western homes, thank you: Charles, Addie, Jessie, Ross, Katherine, and Todd. We love you, and we certainly couldn't have done it without you! —*CRE and AH*

For Charles,
because home is where the heart is.

"Elbow room combined with personal
freedom leads to dangerous enticements.
When land woos us with the power of
creation, it confers on us a mighty
burden. Overnight we must make a
choice that will render us either hero,
rogue, adversary, custodian, or crook."
—JOHN HEMINWAY, *Yonder*

contents

introduction

"Montana is different from other states because it embodies a single, compelling idea. The idea is: open space, sparsely populated. The idea assumes its own life if we situate ourselves at the heart of this aloneness. When each of us first sets foot in Montana, it would appear we can do what we like with the void. We can fill it, we can exploit it, we can restore it, we can leave it alone." —JOHN HEMINWAY, *Yonder*

For most people, what's so special about the West is its immensity, its uplifting views, and the exhilarating feeling of freedom engendered by open space, fresh air, and spectacular scenery. But for me the true West lies not so much in its post-card characteristics as in the myriad details that comprise the western experience: the scent of sage on a hot day; the sound of country music wafting through a horse barn; a glimpse of a border collie waiting, ears pricked, in the back of a pickup; the rifle-pinged "Open Range" signs along rural routes; the clink of spurs on a main street sidewalk; a loaded horse trailer parked outside a bar; the cheerful salute of sunflowers along a country road.

On a country-music-fueled road trip in late May, it's redwing blackbirds swooping low along the roadside on a sunny seventy-five-degree day. As soon as the sun dips behind the mountains it will be wintry cold. The snow-cloaked Absarokas massed to the west remind me that a Montana spring is ephemeral, more a suggestion than a season.

I'm skirting the northwest corner of the eighteen-million-acre Greater Yellowstone Ecosystem, but this could be anywhere in the rural west. There's Fort Rockvale Restaurant, with its thirty-foot-tall metal frontiersman holding his rifle. Old ranch houses are flanked by mature trees clustered against them, planted long ago as buffers to the winds coming across the flat fields extending all around. A derelict homesteader's cabin is bereft of its windows, as well as half the planks on its roof. It shares a field with a newly built overstated log gateway—a symbolic contrast in today's West.

Although some sights seem eternal, change has come rapidly to this New West, as writer Thea Marx poignantly notes. She describes heading out early for a photo shoot just outside Cody, Wyoming. "As the sun came up, so did reality. This picturesque

valley abutting the Absaroka Mountain Range now hosts homes of every shape and size. Plunked into the middle of hay meadows, hovering on the banks of the Shoshone River, and balancing atop the foothills. As a fifth-generation Wyoming ranch girl, my heart aches, for the land is no longer viable production land; it is more valuable as real estate to be subdivided. Ranchers and farmers can no longer afford to work the land. An entire way of life is being eradicated."

Marx's heartfelt sense of loss points to what's needed now in the changing western landscape: an increasingly thoughtful approach to western architecture, design, and living, whether it's realized in sensitively sited new construction, imaginatively repurposed historic structures, old construction updated with environmentally efficient technology, or simply family-friendly western homes that are lovingly maintained and fully utilized. Encouragingly, these types of projects are being seen increasingly throughout the mountain West. Creatively designed, thoughtfully conceived, the new Western homes envisioned here are merely a starting point in preserving the very values that make the mountain West so exhilarating, and so unique.

＊　　　　＊　　　　＊

In the mountain West, man's impacts were minimal for generations. In the second half of the twentieth century, though, they accelerated rapidly, and with lasting consequences.

The earliest inhabitants of the mountain West imposed insignificant impacts on the land. The Native Americans lived in tepees made from natural materials, and, since they moved with the seasons, the land had time to recover between visits. Any lasting impacts look natural in the landscape. A tepee ring, for instance, is simply a number of large rocks arranged in a circle; a corn grinding spot merely a depression in a flat surface of rock; an easily overlooked scattering of obsidian around the base of a rock on a ridgetop indicates that someone sat there looking for game or watching for enemies, and wiled away the time making arrowheads.

Renowned Western architect Jonathan Foote provides a consistently emphatic voice in favor of place-based architecture. The trick, he says, is to "let it become what it wants to become, and what the landscape wants it to be, not what your formal training wants it to be."

From the time of the 1804–1806 Lewis & Clark Expedition until the end of the trapper era in the mid-1800s, construction of permanent structures was limited. One-room log cabins—made of natural materials, located near a water source, and hunkered down out of the wind—blended into the landscape. And the trappers moved seasonally. Though they had maximum impact on the beaver population, they had little impact on the visual landscape. What few structures they left behind would eventually crumble back into the ground, if left undisturbed long enough.

The settlement of the West was slow for the first forty years of European presence, then it accelerated rapidly over the next forty years. It started with the arrival of Mormons in Utah in 1847 and the discovery of gold at Sutter's Mill in 1848, and it was followed in rapid succession by the opening of the overland stage route in 1858, the influx of homesteaders following the passage of the Homestead Act of 1862, the first drive up the Chisholm Trail to Kansas in 1867, the completion of the transcontinental railroad in 1869, and the Battle of the Little Bighorn in 1876. The subjugation of the Native American tribes cleared the final obstacle to the flourishing of settlements, the establishment of remote homesteads, and the founding of vast ranches. By 1890, the U.S. Census formally declared the frontier closed.

Over the next century, and fueled by the increasing use of the automobile, development and immigration continued apace. Today, much of the settled west—towns with traffic lights, big-box retail stores, fast-food joints, and a grid pattern of streets lined with single-family homes separated by lawns, fences, and sidewalks—looks just like the rest of America, with an occasional mountain view, saddle shop, or rodeo grounds as a sort of regional exclamation point.

The wild lands of the American West are still vast and transcendentally beautiful. This cabin's smaller footprint makes sense in the context of its surroundings, and is an appropriate use of the form. "People have lost sight of the wonderful simplicity and the extraordinary scale of these old buildings," says Jonathan Foote. "To try to make them something they're not, they miss the whole content of the old materials and the site and they get caught up in storytelling about the form."

*   *   *

The wild lands of the American West are still vast and still transcendentally beautiful. Antelope still bound across open sagebrush hills along the interstate highways, magpies still flash the white of their wings across rustic fencelines, and bald eagles still winter along the banks of western rivers. But the wildest parts of the West are virtual islands, encroached upon on all sides by human development. Grizzly bears and wolves thrive in some areas, but clashes with humans are inevitable—and inevitably escalating. When confrontations do occur, the animal is relocated or destroyed. Forest fires, from the wilds of Montana to the densely populated suburbs of Los Angeles, are increasingly destructive due to development in traditional fire zones and the expansion of suburbs into former ranchlands and open hills. Yet the expansion continues apace, only temporarily slowed by vagaries in the economy.

New structures taking agricultural forms strive to fit into the landscape while speaking to the region's farming and ranching heritage.

Although aquifers are being depleted, open land is being lost to development, wildlife is being stressed, and streambeds are being degraded throughout the West, promising trends are emerging. Responsible valley-wide planning, a move toward quality over quantity in homebuilding, the growing recognition of the value of historic preservation and the creative re-use of existing buildings and materials, and a progressive use of sustainable-design techniques are all discernible trends. Clearly, there's a wish among old-timers and newcomers alike to preserve what is special.

Land planning in Sun Valley, Idaho, for instance, has come a long way in the past decade, explains Scott Boettger. Director of the Wood River Land Trust for the past ten years, his concentration has evolved significantly from his initial mandate to secure conservation easements to protect open space and wildlife. "We've been successful with landowners and easements, and it allows us to say, 'We've done this part. Now, how does it fit into the whole?' Because our limitations are also our benefits. There's only so much precipitation per year, for instance. If we overdevelop, we collapse. We've had to get people thinking about larger impacts. All our communities are going to reach their carrying capacity. All are going to

Asks Scott Boettger, director of the Wood River Land Trust, "How do we build for a sustainable future but also preserve history and wildlife and not deplete the aquifer?" The answer lies in thoughtful, sensitive development.

looking for ways to grow while protecting what's important.

"Without proper planning," Boettger continues, "there's a negative reaction to development. How can we change [that attitude] to build for a sustainable future, but also preserve history and wildlife and not deplete the aquifer? We need to find innovative ways to preserve what we really love without destroying it. It's the hardest thing to do, because it takes the cooperation of everyone."

Historic preservation, in addition to being the ultimate form of recycling, plays a crucial role in preserving regional flavor while minimizing impacts on the environment. Richard Moe, president of the National Trust for Historic Preservation, explains, "Today, we understand that maintaining tangible contact with our past strengthens the sense of stability and continuity that is essential in a healthy society, so we make the preservation of familiar landmarks a key component in the revitalization of neighborhoods and communities that are attractive and livable. It's all about bringing us together, encouraging us to recognize the shared heritage that defines and unites us as a nation and a people."

For every example of a salvaged homestead or repurposed historic structure in these pages, there are hundreds more across the

West: train stations, grain elevators, mercantiles, and one-room schoolhouses. There's a beauty and integrity in these structures that can't easily be replicated, yet for the past few decades much homebuilding emphasis, particularly for second homes, has been on volume rather than appropriateness. "People have lost sight of the wonderful simplicity and the extraordinary scale of these old buildings," says master architect Jonathan Foote. "In trying to make them something they're not, they miss the whole content of the old materials and the site and they get caught up in story-telling about the form." The result, he says, "is a streaking toward the rococo."

Foote advocates place-based architecture. Whether the forms are rustic or modern, their design should begin and be guided by the site. "What drew me to the West," he says, "were the home-steader cabins in the middle of nowhere, and the fences that are falling down. They tie in beautifully with musical imagery and poetic imagery." The challenge, he explains, is to allow architecture to happen organically. "If you let that happen, you can avoid destroying the very thing you've come for."

Forward-thinking developers are providing more and better in-town living options while pre-serving the architectural fabric of their communities. A former cigar factory in down-town Livingston, Montana, was sensitively restored as industrial-chic condominium apartments.

Across the West, individuals are making a difference in educating and leading by example. Architect Lori Ryker, an authority in sustainable design, founded a nonprofit organization called the Artemis Institute to walk emergent architects through the process of building in harmony with nature. The program combines architectural studies with environmental philosophy and backcountry experiences; it culminates in the hands-on building of a structure that is low impact and site-appropriate.

"When we talk and write about architecture, we most often talk and write about the object, divorced from its nature, its place," says Ryker. "Perhaps this way of talking produces a subsequent way of thinking and designing that fails to consider the depth and power, value and necessity of place. Failing to consider place, we not only fail to consider the qualities of the landscape and terrestrial environment but we also fail to consider people, their social and cultural influences, and the living condition of what we make."

Patty Agnew, a Montana sheep rancher and artist, helped write Sweetgrass County's Code of the West, a pamphlet about living and building in the mountain West for new landowners in the county. It demystifies such topics as subsurface mineral rights and fire protection, points out that the area's average rainfall is only twelve inches per year, and tactfully suggests that in any new construction the landowner consider river and stream setbacks, viewshed preservation, light pollution, and architectural compatibility.

It often is simply a case of education, she says; if people make decisions too quickly, before getting to know the area and its issues, such as high winds or mudslides, they may regret their choices. For instance, Agnew points out, "Most people come from places with trees. They don't think about the viewshed. Tucking new homes into the landscape is one way to protect the value of your investment and the integrity of the community."

Individuals too are making thoughtful decisions as to their own contribution to the fabric of the community in which they live. Doug Tedrow, an artisan furniture maker in Idaho, owns the smallest lot in Ketchum. He chose to blend in when he hand-built his new home. "It's board-and-batten, and I came up with a stain that simulates weathered gray. I used rusty bolts and rusted attic vents," he says of his brand new home. "I wanted people to drive by and say, 'Look at that little old house. What a cool old house.'"

Whether the homes are new built to look old, old structures that have been repurposed, historic homes that have been lovingly maintained, or modern designs embracing the latest in sustainable-design techniques, the new Western homes featured here strive for appropriateness, each in its own way. The ultimate goal should be homes that sit lightly on the land. The examples are innumerable, the possibilities inspiring.

"It's board-and-batten, and I came up with a stain that simulates weathered gray. I used rusty bolts and rusted attic vents. I wanted people to drive by and say, 'Look at that little old house. What a cool old house.'"

A post-and-beam barn home—set high in the hills above an old dairy farm yet still tucked into the land—makes the most of its setting. On a clear day the views reach all the way to the coast. "The word 'spiritual' is overused these days," says the owner, "but it's without question a spiritual place. The more you're there, the less you want to leave. My ambition is to buy food for a month and never go out."

post-and-beam rustic chic

California's fabled Marin County has long been defined by its stunning vistas of mountains, ocean, and bay, and its rugged, scenic beaches, still pristine despite their proximity to San Francisco. But perhaps its most striking characteristic is its undeveloped open space. Approximately 70 percent of the county is protected. While much of that comprises the Golden Gate National Recreation Area and Point Reyes National Seashore, Muir Beach, Muir Woods, and Mount Tamalpais State Park, a vast amount of conserved land lies in the county's interior; surprisingly, this is cattle-ranch and dairy-farm country.

Twenty-five years ago, an Englishman residing in California was spending the day in Sonoma, where he owned some property. "I wasn't looking to buy," he recalls, "but I happened to pick up a free brochure. And I happened to put it on the seat of my car. And I happened to see an ad on the back of the brochure. . . . I called the realtor and asked, 'Is it pretty?' and he said, 'It's beautiful.' And the minute he said that, I knew."

The land, 270 acres of dramatic open high hills, oak woodland, bay-leaf-scented forest, and its own hidden valley with a large pond at its center, was awash in wildlife, draped by coastal fog, and accessed through a rustic old dairy ranch. The owner still vividly recalls his first impression. "I took one step onto the property and said, 'I'll buy it.'

"Originally I couldn't afford a house," he continues, "so we built a classic redwood barn. It was very, very bare bones. At first we lived in an Airstream trailer; then we had the barn and lived upstairs with no running water. But once we had a baby we decided we needed a proper house."

Contractor Tyler Shelton, who had designed and built the original post-and-beam structure, returned to fit out the interior walls and plumbing. Designer Caroline "Rossi" Scott, a compatriot and close friend of the owner's, was brought in to conceive and execute the interior design. Together the three determined the home's layout and proportions. "We sat down and sketched around a table," recalls Rossi. "It was really a brainstorming session about how [the owner] likes to live, and how to create a functional space. It was a joint effort; that's the way I do a lot of my projects. The client needs to be involved," she adds, "because at the end of the day, they'll be the ones living there."

The process of turning a barn into a home was dictated by the proportions of the existing structure, and the desire of both

The home's signature style is uncluttered simplicity, with a nod to designer Rossi Scott's upbringing in Scotland. "I found the armchair in the Petaluma antiques market," she recalls. She had it covered in velvet—the deep plum color is "very Scottish," she says— and had the arms and legs silver-leafed by Jafe Refinishers in San Francisco.

A concrete mantel over steel doors is crowned simply by mounted stag antlers. White upholstery creates a clean look, while luxurious angora hides over two ottomans offer a cozy place to curl up in front of the fire. The bold dash of orange on the opposite walls, says the designer, was "a very simple way of getting that element of surprise without having to paint the whole room."

designer and client to retain the look of a barn, rather than turning it into a house. "What I enjoyed most," recalls the owner, "was the discipline of building twelve by twelve, and the discipline of working with the post and beams. Everyone I know makes the kitchen too big," he adds, "but twelve by twelve is the right size."

"Because the barn existed," explains Rossi, "it very much spoke for itself." Thus, two bedrooms and a bath naturally lined up along one wall; she kept the windows on that side small enough to retain the barn look when viewed from the approach to the house. (For the same reason, there are dormers only on the back side of the structure.) On either end of the barn, slightly larger windows open up to the spectacular views, while on the far wall—away from the approach, but overlooking the private valley—floor-to-ceiling glass doors open up to nature, allowing indoors and outdoors to merge.

The large mirror,
with its layers of
midnight blue
lacquer, was
designed by Rossi
Scott. It brings light
indoors and reflects
the surrounding
landscape.

Most of the ground floor is given over to one large dining/
living/cooking space. "The idea was to have the main living area
as spacious as possible," says Rossi. "I wasn't going to waste floor
space on the bedrooms." The upstairs is one large master bedroom
suite, with a spacious spa-like bath, a sofa, and a children's bed
tucked under the eaves.

Beyond its extraordinary setting, the most striking aspect of
the home is its simplicity, the feeling of spaciousness despite its
small footprint, and the fact that notwithstanding the streamlined,
almost ascetic décor, the space is both cozy and inviting.

"I'd been brought up in Scotland," explains the designer.
"The way I design is what I grew up with. I like that homey ranch
feel, but not clutter. If you go to a proper hunting or fishing lodge
in Scotland, you have your antlers, you have your sheepskin. You
have white, white walls and on one wall perhaps hundreds of
antlers, with a sofa underneath and maybe a table, and that's it.
It's almost like art."

Open stainless-steel shelving gives the kitchen a light and airy feeling and keeps the look more informal and natural, says the designer. "And the exposed beams help keep the feeling of being in a barn."

The effect of the home is achieved through its interplay of surfaces, textures and color—wood ceilings and beams, concrete floors, white walls and chairs, minimal furniture, a couple of throw rugs, and a blast of orange on one wall. A western sense of place is conveyed through sheepskins covering the ottoman and thrown over the backs of armchairs, hats hung along the stairway landing, and deer antlers mounted over the fireplace. By day nature retains center stage; by night, the fireplace is the focal point, with candles and strategic lighting enhancing the feeling of warmth and intimacy.

Upstairs, the space is functional but still spare, with mostly white furnishings and textiles; there, nature is the most important aspect of the decor. "The top rooms have the most amazing views," explains the designer. "That's why there are no blinds. At night the stars are in your room and the moon comes up over the hills. You hear the owls on top of the roof and the coyotes in the distance. At five a.m. you have the fog in your bedroom. It's just the most amazing place to wake up."

Shortly after collaborating with shipwright's carpenters to refurbish an antique yacht, the designer worked with craftsman Paul Reffell to conceive the master bedroom cupboards. "I didn't want to break up the room," she explains. "So I did cupboards under the eaves, like a yacht's."

The lesson inherent in this coastal California ode to rustic modernism is the importance of respecting the land. The more elaborate the house, Rossi Scott points out, the more that is taken away from the experience of living within nature.

"There's nothing complicated about this barn," she says. "I don't like to create drama where there is none. It's very simple: form follows function. And it works. You have your necessities: fireplace, kitchen, bath, and an enormous bedroom upstairs. What more do you need, really? If there's too much going on the jackrabbits wouldn't be so tame, and the bobcat wouldn't come up to the front door, and the eagles wouldn't nest there. Ultimately it belongs to nature, and we're nature's guests."

"I like symmetry," says the designer. "And with the white tile it's very simple. I try to keep it ageless."

The more elaborate the house, the more that is taken away from the experience of living within nature.

The mythical West is
alive and well in
the remote valleys
and box canyons
surrounding Yellow-
stone National Park.
A Montana ranch
on a swift-flowing
river carries the
weight of history in
its log lodge and
outbuildings. Its
owners think of
themselves as
custodians of a
rich legacy.

a cycle of enchantment

The mountain West is in some ways akin to a grand public trust. There are vast swaths of high desert managed for oil, gas, cattle, and timber by the Bureau of Land Management; hundreds of thousands of acres of national forests, with their designated wilderness areas; countless state parks and beaches; unique national monuments, and immense national parks (Yellowstone alone is more than four million acres). The myth of the West derives not just from the grandeur of the scenery and the feeling of freedom its open space engenders, but from the notion of all that untrammeled roadless wilderness—and the captivating idea that at any moment one can simply disappear into nature.

The most coveted bits of this mythical west—the notion of "West" that explains why the New York investment banker or L.A. producer keeps cowboy boots in the back of her closet, counts the days until his dude-ranch vacation, or pays for the privilege of enduring the dust and heat of a cattle drive—are privately owned slices of western heaven. These legendary bits of acreage, spring-fed or river-irrigated, blessed with river bottom and hay meadows and mature cottonwoods and aspens, wild with big game, and euphoric with views, are magical for their close proximity to an access point into the heart of the wilderness. Whether one actually hikes, backpacks or takes pack trips into the high country is not the point. The point is simply knowing that one can head into the wilderness, can disappear over the nearest pass and not see a road or sign of civilization for weeks.

Despite all of today's high-tech conveniences, such places, the scenic valleys and box canyons abutting the wilderness, are still remote—hence their enduring appeal. They can be hazardous to reach, even in summer; some are inaccessible in winter. It makes

Rooms open into rooms in this rambling lodge building. Classic western interiors make use of exposed wood, stone fireplaces, Edward Curtis photographs, and Native American rugs.

A multitude of interesting artifacts speak to the layers of history at the Bar 20 Ranch. Owner John Heminway became captive to the mystery of those who had lived in and loved the ranch before him; he dug deep into the property's history and ultimately wrote the book *Yonder* about his quest.

one wonder, then, about those hardy souls who chose to carve out homes in these places in the decades after the turn of the century. To pass by an old homesteader's cabin is to imagine the early settlers' lives, to try to visualize the reality of a family of four sharing a one-room cabin. To spend time at an old dude ranch is to wonder what those early ranchers' lives were like, to ponder what drove them and why they left. Were they irresistibly drawn to the grandeur of the place, or were they running away from something?

When in the mid-1980s documentary filmmaker John Heminway and his sister, celebrated designer Hilary Heminway, first discovered the West Fork of the Boulder River, hidden and almost inaccessible in the wild precipitous folds of mountains north of Yellowstone National Park, they were astounded by its glorious scenery and its back-of-beyond quality. (The only clear part of the

The Bar 20 bedrooms are simple and comfortable, exactly as they should be in a remote historic setting. The owner has written books and documentaries in his compact book-lined study.

original directions they'd been given, Hilary Heminway recalls, was, "Turn right at the Road Kill Café.") And when they first glimpsed the Bar 20 Ranch, its bunkhouses, barn, and main house of logs, they had an immediate and atavistic sensation of belonging.

The main structure wasn't picturesque in the usual sense, writes John Heminway in his book *Yonder*. "Shingles had blown from the roof across the patchy lawn; the building's porches sagged, and a mountain chickadee lay dead beneath a crudely installed picture window. The Bar 20 was certainly no trophy home; it boasted no cathedral ceiling, no great room, no hot tub, and the marauding aspens denied what every house should have—a breathtaking view." Yet there was something about the way it fit into the landscape, the river in the foreground flowing wide and shallow, remarkably clear over rounded glacial stones, and sheltering limestone cliffs rising up behind, that drew them in and held them. Within four months, the property was theirs.

As they set about repairing the roof, clearing out mouse droppings, and installing furnishings, John Heminway over time became entranced not just by the place but by its story. From the first glimpse upon descending the hill to the river bottom, to the ratcheting sound both car and boots make when crossing the old bridge, to the tantalizing glimpse of the log barn nestled in its own

A screened porch with banquet-sized dining table offers all the benefits of the outdoors—without the mosquitos.

clearing, Bar 20 exudes character. There one can feel the weight of history and sense that the valley still carries the spirit of generations of itinerants and inhabitants who, over the course of more than one hundred years, gazed upon the same view, rode among the same trees, and heard the same river flowing over glacial stones every morning upon waking.

Yonder chronicles Heminway's captivation by a simple sheaf of papers, handed to him without explanation by the previous owner as he departed the valley for the last time. The series of scribbled notations, some indecipherable, marked random moments of the Bar 20's history. Heminway was drawn to the papers as clues to a mystery; he felt driven to reconstruct the ranch's past. The more the author uncovered, the deeper he dug, until he'd pieced together the truths of his predecessors. He wished to understand as closely as he could the "cycle of enchantment" of which he was now irretrievably a player. And ultimately he succeeded in chronicling the history of the ranch, from the early Shoshone Indians, followed by small bands of the Mountain Crow, to the first homesteader (rights granted in 1902), to the long residency of Stanley and Lucille Cox, a fastidious eastern couple who tried to market the Bar 20 as an upscale dude ranch—and stayed, seemingly unhappily, for two decades.

A tepee, firepit, and a structure called "Skunk House" all contribute rustic charm to the ranch's unique character.

INFORMATION

*   *   *

As he took possession of the main Bar 20 Ranch, and his sister the log home up on the hill with the view up the valley, Heminway made it his own while honoring its past, ever mindful of those who came before. The result is a hushed quality in rooms that carry the weight of history in a valley characterized by its feeling of timelessness.

The main lodge—old logs, stone chimney, green trim—is snugged down, seemingly rooted in the earth. It is comfortable and welcoming, quiet but not oppressive. It has porches with rustic railings and hanging flowerpots, a long, narrow screened-in porch filled with wicker furniture, throw rugs, old painted furniture, and a dog bed. Hummingbirds flit past, their wings thrumming over the sound of trickling water from a rustic fountain that doubles as a horse trough.

Inside, low-ceilinged rooms open each to the next, each unique and draped in the past in multiple layers of art, collectibles, furnishings, and artifacts. In the entry area, a dining table with built-in benches is crowned by an arrangement of ten antique fish prints. Coats, hats, and creels hang by the door. A primitive painting of a man and dog hangs over a stone fireplace; beaded gauntlet gloves lie on the mantel. Bedrooms have mosquito-netted beds and wood-burning stoves set against pressed-tin backdrops.

Country antiques in whimsical arrangements make for authentic western interiors in this retro-cool bunkhouse.

The kitchen features an old range, a corner table with built-in seating, open shelves of irregularly stacked china plates, and blue-and-white painted cupboards. The log-beamed living room is intimately scaled, with textured carpets, throw rugs, leather-covered ceilings, and a suite of original Edward Curtis photographs—some original, some placed by the Heminway siblings in the early days of ranch ownership and some added more recently by Heminway's wife, an art collector whose touch has never tampered with history but subtly enhanced it.

Stacks of vintage Pendleton blankets, a coffee table fashioned from an old chicken coop, comfortable seating, interesting books, and a ceiling covered with deer skins give designer Hilary Heminway's Grouse House a layered, lived-in look.

A quiet reading corner features an antique rocker, a red-leather-upholstered chair and fringed ottoman, a Chinese lamp, a squirrel nut cracker, and vintage oil paintings of the mountain West, often referred to as "Sunday paintings."

Guest cabins, a small office, bunkhouses, and a darkly weathered log barn, its box stalls and small tack room purely functional, round out the encampment shared by the Heminway siblings. Just uphill and downriver is Hilary Heminway's rustic home, Grouse House. There the designer painted the logs green, changed the layout slightly without expanding the homes' original footprint, and decorated the home with "junkyard-treasures-meet-western-make-do," cast-offs rehabilitated in the hands of a master. Wooden chairs with linoleum seats, handpainted by Heminway and friends, a chicken incubator turned into a coffee table, a collection of windmill weights, vintage Pendleton blankets, old western books, tables from Yellowstone Park, and rustic

Grouse House's two bedrooms are timeless. The master bedroom, its handpainted bed crowned by a gathered drapery of mosquito netting, features a wood-stove backed by pressed tin painted turquoise. "I had to use tractor paint," says Heminway. "It doesn't come in very many colors."

furniture designed by Heminway and crafted by her artisan pals create comfortable, quirky interiors. But at Grouse House, as at the Bar 20, the main event is the view, the valley, all of the outdoors.

And the outdoors is ever present, even indoors, says Hilary Heminway. "It's camp living. You live with critters in the house— mice, packrats, weasels, and moles. We try to tell them to go back outside. Out there," she adds, "are elk, moose, deer, sandhill cranes, bears, and wolves."

Deeply committed to the preservation of the valley, and ever mindful of their role as stewards of a special place, both Heminways feel the weight of history and their responsibility to it. "Our intention at the Bar 20," writes John Heminway, "was to build not a stately home but to preserve an old place's integrity, however fugitive. We had fallen under the spell of a river and a set of buildings: we were smitten by its logs."

A cozy reading nook in a bunk-house features handmade pillows, deer-hide draperies, and vintage Pendleton blankets.

An environmentally sensitive family compound on the banks of the Yellowstone River presented challenging design considerations for architect Lori Ryker. She adapted two existing structures to make way for the river, the wildlife, and even the mature cottonwood tree that grows through the deck.

new west
fishing cabin

Lori Ryker's path from Harvard's Graduate School of
Architecture and Texas A&M University's PhD program
landed her in rural Montana ten years ago. An architecture
professor who has authored two books on off-the-grid sustainable homes, Ryker has given plenty of thought to the question
of how to build and live responsibly in the world's most beautiful places, despite the unavoidable conundrum inherent in
that prospect: that building in pristine places, by definition,
impacts the environment.

In 2003 Ryker founded the nonprofit Artemis Institute,
she explains, as a way of offering architects-in-training the
opportunity "to help them better understand their relationship
and responsibility to the natural world, and to understand
how nature inspires and influences their educational process.
Out of that," she says, "comes a connection to sustainability."

A home designed by Ryker for herself, with architect Brett Nave, is set in open grassland hills near Livingston, Montana. The contemporary ranch home is made of high-tech eco-conscious materials (no-toxicity spray-in insulation, for instance), combined with local raw materials (such as Douglas fir harvested just thirty miles away). Built low and sensitively sited, the home is virtually invisible to its neighbors. Its water catchments, geothermal heating system, solar panel grid, and garden of native trees and grasses attest to its practical conscientiousness, while its interplay of polished concrete, recycled steel, exposed wood, and natural light create comfortable, livable interiors that still make the most of the natural setting.

While her projects may redefine the idea of western vernacular, they are, at heart, all about connecting to the land. "An architect, like most artists, has a great responsibility to society, because they are the people that help create culture," Ryker explains. "When I look around in the world, it seems like there's a great schism, or disconnect, to appreciating and understanding the natural world."

In a recent project Ryker completed for a multigenerational family, the natural world took a particularly dynamic form. A forty-acre parcel on the banks of the Yellowstone River demanded a thoughtful, practical approach to the issue of nature's vagaries—as well as a creative response to strict county floodway regulations. The clients, a mother and father, their daughter, and her two children, were looking for a piece of land "for a casual family compound so they could spend time together in Montana fishing, skiing, and spending holidays together," Ryker explains.

The site's position on the river was a great attraction but also represented its greatest limitations. An existing structure—"a typical rancher-built thing, one room that had been added onto; not

A modernist interior speaks to its setting through natural fibers, a tree stump side table and plenty of windows to bring in the natural world.

dilapidated but not in great shape," says Ryker—was tackled first. "We basically stripped the house inside and out and tried to bring back its Montana character, though rendered in a more contemporary way, mainly through materials."

An old chicken shack was next, Ryker recalls. "We took the roof off and made it taller. We turned it into a fishing cabin, with two sets of twin beds, a kitchenette, and a great set of windows looking out toward the river."

The Yellowstone River, one of the very few undammed rivers in the lower forty-eight states, has little respect for private property and freely breaches its banks during flood season. When the implications of existing floodway restrictions became clear to the clients, Ryker recalls, "We realized we couldn't build on the river's edge. So we built on existing foundations. (Luckily there were foundations," she adds. "A lot of cabins in Montana are logs sitting on rocks.) We stayed within the foundation's footprint, then improved it and put it on stilts so [the building] wouldn't be destroyed. We knew the house would be small, but that was fine.

A small central gathering space offers plenty of seating options yet still invokes intimacy.

They were there to be outside, not to sit in their house."

The structure—two "cabin boxes," one a master-bedroom suite and one a living room with loft—was designed as a western interpretation of a southern "dogtrot," where two enclosed spaces are situated to create a middle space, which then becomes an open porch. This porch accommodates an unusual feature: a mature cottonwood grows right through the deck. A breezeway with doors on either side houses the dining table. "The family can open the doors to allow the breeze to come through," Ryker explains, "which is useful in August when it's 103 degrees. And they can move the family life out onto the porch when the weather is great. By putting the structure up on stilts, the building is high enough to see into the river."

By orienting the structures thoughtfully, Ryker made the most of their placement. "The site can be quite windy," she explains. "The elevated cabin is oriented with the narrow side to the wind, with fewer openings on that side. There are larger openings to the

Open shelving in the kitchen and ottoman seating in place of high-backed dining chairs declutter high-use spaces.

"A lot of thought goes into where the sun is coming from and where the wind is coming from— both to reduce energy usage and to open up to the natural world."

A master bedroom with windows placed high looking out into the trees offers a private refuge.

southwest, where the prevailing summer breezes come from. The deciduous trees mean that the house is heavily shaded in the summer. But the house gets great sunlight in the winter months with the colder weather.

"When I'm designing," she adds, "a lot of thought goes into where the sun is coming from and where the wind is coming from—both to reduce energy usage and to open up to the natural world. Architecture should include you in the landscape rather than exclude you from it."

Central to this approach is a resistance to grooming every bit of wild land. Of the site's almost forty available acres, only four show any sign of human interference. Consequently, the property, despite its proximity to town, is awash in wildlife: moose, elk, deer, black bear, and waterfowl.

Building in moderation and with thoughtful planning, and landscaping in a restrained manner, is practical, cost-effective, and environmentally sensitive. But it also creates a feeling of intimacy and a closeness to nature, both indoors and out.

"Smaller spaces are very intimate," says Lori Ryker. "You don't get lost inside the house, and you're always close to the perimeter. You always feel the breezes coming through, so there's a sense of nature at all times. When you design sensitively," she adds, "it ties you to the natural world."

Mid-century minimalism in a western interior makes the most of the quiet interplay of natural light.

A stone and timber dwelling designed by Larry Pearson of Pearson Design Group sits high up in the mountains at an elevation of 8,700 feet. Its hand-crafted door—handmade by Dan Pittenger and Tim Sutherland from drawings by Shelby Rose—is one tactile example of the fine craftsmanship found throughout the structure.

rustic mountain house

Without the presence of mountains—as vertically soaring backdrop or distant snow-capped scenery—the western range would just be so much arid open space. Big Sky country is lent magnitude by the massing of peaks on the periphery of that vast blue arc. The concept of Big Sky is, quite simply, endless overarching firmament. But without the mountains to lend perspective, one has no sense of just how big it is.

In the early days, practically minded settlers built on the flats or tucked their homesteads into draws, out of the wind, near a water source and in places from which they could still get out on horseback after a snowfall. But a few of the most adventurous, and profit-minded, headed into the mountains. They built cabins up high in the wilderness, taking their chances with weather, wolves, and grizzlies in pursuit of precious metals, furs, and beaver pelts.

A log cabin in the mountains is an archetypal American form, a symbol of retreat, refuge, and a rugged independent lifestyle. While today's high-elevation cabin dwellers are more likely to be seeking thrills on the ski slopes than snowshoeing through drifts to check their trap lines, the cabin enduringly represents a compact shelter from the elements. The concept is sturdy, solid construction anchored by a fireplace or wood stove and given weight by the trees that created it, which also serve to tie it to its setting. The cabin blends into the landscape and is snug and solid; it is not likely to shudder in the wind or buckle under snow mass.

A high-elevation site near Big Sky, Montana, offered spectacular views as well as the usual challenges—steep slope, extreme altitude, heavy snowfall in winter—to longtime Bozeman architect Larry Pearson and his project managers Shelby Rose and Jed Thomas. Pearson is a multifaceted designer, but he is best known for expressive rustic style: massive hand-hewn timbers, locally quarried stones, artisan-crafted metal- and woodwork, and vaulted-ceilinged spaces for multiple generations to gather while reveling in the mountain lifestyle.

Pearson was given free rein by his client-partners to design a unique rustic ski lodge that makes the most of its setting—a sloping wooded draw with a natural water source that looks out toward Cedar and Pioneer Mountains and offers tantalizing glimpses into designated wilderness areas. The setting, at an elevation of 8,700 feet, is true high country. "There are high alpine lake basins and grizzly bears," says Pearson. "It's the real western alpine experience."

The home's three stories are built into the hillside, a technique that simultaneously reduces heat loss and minimizes bulk; its rustic exterior guarantees that from a distance it blends into the environment. Careful siting amongst tall pines with a mountain rising

A massive stone fireplace, stepped at its base with irregularly jutting stones at its top, anchors the home inside and out while creating a vertical element that ties the three levels together.

The vaulted-ceilinged great room opens into the dining area and kitchen, where ceilings are lower, creating more intimate spaces for cooking and dining by candlelight under an antler chandelier made by local craftsman Frank Long.

abruptly behind further veils the structure from long-distance view. A massive fireplace, stepped at its base with jutting-sky-ward irregular stones at its top, anchors the home inside and out while creating a vertical element that ties the three levels together. Covered log breezeways linking the guesthouse, with its stone tower, to the main house force the visitor into nature while still providing shelter from the elements.

A visitor's first interaction with the house is a tactile one. The handmade rustic door, with locally crafted wrought-iron hinges and handle, opens to a modestly scaled entry hall, with an inviting bench for removing snowy boots tucked under stairs leading up to the home's main volume. One then ascends into the living room, the architect explains. "You come in from below onto the main floor and the view opens up." This view comprises not just the spectacular scenery out the windows but the soaring great room centered on the impressive fireplace. "The bigger the view, the greater the need to anchor the house," explains Pearson. "The fireplace holds the house to the hill and matches the hill in its strength."

As in many western houses, this central gathering space is the heart of the home. "Many of our clients are driven to a central larger space for the family to come together," says Pearson. "It's a social hub, usually larger, vaulted, and more dramatic. I love the contrast of a larger space with many more intimate spaces, such as a low-ceilinged den or library. It sets up the experience for winter and summer use.

In keeping with the family-friendly feeling of casual open-ness, the living room is open to the dining room and kitchen. "One thing we've found in recreational cabins," Pearson explains, "is that everything is shared space. You don't have the living room closed off from the dining room closed off

from the kitchen. The kitchen needs to be beautiful, and it needs to visually connect to the living areas." If the living room is the heart of the home, he adds, "the kitchen is the hub."

The central gathering spot centered on the fireplace and open to the kitchen and dining rooms; the master suite and quiet office space; the private guest quarters removed from foot traffic; the children's bedrooms; the mudroom and the wine cellar—these are the elements that compose today's family lodge. All other amenities are found just outside the door, in the vast wilderness playground that is the mountain West.

In times of rampant development, increased resource depletion, and environmental impacts from new construction, building in a wilderness setting carries certain obligations. "So many people grew up spending time in the national parks. Many people, like me, had indelible experiences in their youths," Pearson reflects. "How do you convey those experiences to the next generation, and create a touchstone to the past? This is a legacy

The interplay of textures and lighting sources create warm interiors in what Pearson calls a "legacy property" which will pass on environmental aesthetics and appreciation for the wilderness from one generation to the next.

"Here, we're actually in the Yellowstone
                ecosystem; it's the same pristine
wilderness. We're trying to take
                (this sense of) responsibility and
aesthetic values into architecture."

A master bath features wide-plank flooring, hand-hewn towel hooks, open shelving, and a "tub with a view" into the surrounding wilderness areas.

property, passing on a value from one generation to the next. Here, we're actually in the Yellowstone ecosystem; it's the same pristine wilderness. We're trying to take [this sense of] responsibility and aesthetic values into architecture."

With this heightened awareness, Pearson strives for an environmental conscientiousness in his projects. "It may look like a highly detailed log home, but it has incredible insulation systems, and it has the highest-tech setback thermostat and boiler designs. It has a significant amount of south-facing glass, which corresponds to the views. It's very sensitive and it does perform very well, yet still carries traditional values. And traditional values," Pearson says, "are why people come to Montana."

A collection of well-worn cowboy hats and an antique "God Bless Our Home" sampler convey a warm welcome in this classic ranch entry hall and mudroom.

homes on the range

The Upper South Fork of Wyoming's Shoshone River, south-west of Cody, hasn't changed much in the past century. It's been protected by its remoteness and its topography. An hour's drive from the nearest convenience store, it is almost entirely surrounded by the Shoshone National Forest, with five major trailheads spiraling outward into the rugged, precipitous Washakie Wilderness. From the Upper South Fork, it's as close to Dubois as it is to Cody—but traveling horseback, pulling a pack sting, it's a much slower trip.

Pickups are the vehicle of choice, with or without a horse trailer in tow. Windshields are often cracked, because the last ten miles of road are unpaved. Those last ten miles are open cattle range, though in winter it's not cattle the drivers need to dodge but elk and bighorn sheep. Spring and summer, grizzlies drop down out of the upper drainages and roam along the river corridor, stopping at ranches along the way. In May and June—when the cow elk are still calving down in the valley—neighbors call each other to report of grizzly movements: the sow with three cubs that's known to be aggressive charged a guy taking a picture from across the river, one rancher reports; the sow with the twin cubs who's know to be mild-mannered wandered through the Johnsons' yard, and she and the cubs are now headed downriver. Another rancher describes finding claw marks across the hindquarters of two of his horses: mountain lion, maybe?

Between winter blizzards, spring mudslides, summer thunderstorms, and fall wildfires, it's a community of ranches that have to neighbor well and take care of their own. Good fences make good neighbors, and a rancher might become inflamed when someone else's cows repeatedly end up in his hay meadows. But in a serious situation they all come together at the drop of a cowboy hat.

Three ranches on both sides of the river capture a different valley past while expressing their own unique histories and needs: The Mariposa, a gathering place for four generations of an extended family; Ishawooa Creek Ranch, one hundred acres stretched along the river with only an old guest cabin from a historic dude ranch up the road for lodging; and the EJ, a 1931 homestead and trapper's cabin, added onto over the years and fitted out with barns and outbuildings.

A glass doorway opens into an inviting hall where hefty logs, an M.C. Poulsen oil painting, a half-round table by Cody artisan Lester Santos, and a Navajo rug cast a warm glow.

A 1950s-era living
room remains
untouched in a
recent renovation,
a tribute to previous
generations who
lived on—and
loved—the
Mariposa Ranch.

the mariposa

The Mariposa Ranch consists of several hundred acres of foothills, cottonwood trees, and hay meadows irrigated by Ishawooa Creek where it tumbles out of the national forest, clear, fast, and full of trout. Log buildings from the 1940s constitute the heart of the ranch, whose structures have been added onto over the years with guest cabins, a large functional horse barn, and a wood frame "fun barn" filled with funky western furniture, taxidermy mounts, an old upright piano, and vintage memorabilia such as an 1890s 3-by-5-foot black-and-white photograph of the entire cast of performers, mounted horseback, hats in outstretched hands, of Buffalo Bill's Wild West Show.

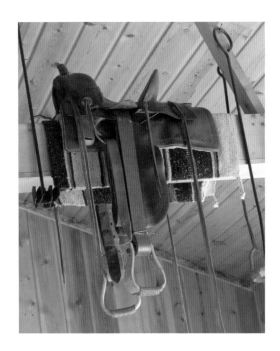

While some structures have been left untouched, the main lodge was completely rebuilt after the current owners acquired the ranch a decade ago. A labyrinth of rooms when purchased, the structure was opened up and reproportioned. All rooms were furnished with western furniture and metalwork by local artisans, each piece commissioned by and designed in collaboration with the owners, dedicated patrons of Wyoming's artists. The walls were hung with paintings purchased by the couple, who go beyond simply buying art to following the careers of the artists they collect; many of them they count as friends. A generously proportioned kitchen and dining room were built and positioned to maximize the spectacular views of the sheer cliffs across the valley. Large open decks with comfortable furniture and overflowing flower boxes now offer the perfect vantage point for enjoying the day's last rays of sunshine as they color the cliffs a rosy pink.

Only one room, the original sunken living room, was left untouched—at the husband's emphatic request. The room is a slice in time, a monument to a bygone era of the 1950s West: its stone fireplace, the mantel cluttered with skulls, bones, antlers,

The dining great room doubles as a cozy place to read by the fire. Three tables designed by the owner and made by a local artisan can be put together for multi-generational family gatherings. Doors to an expansive deck give way to glorious views across the valley.

birds' nests, and other organic litter of the plains; its beams, not log but utilitarian 4 x 8s, hung with southwestern saddle blankets and western saddles and flanked by branding irons hanging from the ceiling; its wildlife mounts, all hunted in the surrounding forests; and its eclectic mix of furniture, including a Victorian-look black leather love seat. Here the adults might sit by the fire with a book on a rainy evening while the grandchildren play with board games and toys—a cozy refuge indeed after a day spent out in the elements.

As the owners' family expanded, the three-bedroom main lodge and several cabins began to overflow with grandchildren in the summer. Over time, as the musical-bedroom game became tiresome and the need for a quiet place to run the family business became more pressing, the owners cast about for an appropriate site to build a retreat for themselves. Eager to capitalize on the extraordinary views across and down the valley but conscious of the neighbor's right to not have to view the structure, the couple designed a mountainside aerie of log and glass designed to disappear into the hillside far above Ishawooa Creek.

The newly constructed one-bedroom cabin is compact yet has a feeling of spaciousness in its living room/dining area and its entry hall with hand-crafted details.

The one-bedroom home features a spacious entry hall that opens into a combined kitchen/living/dining area whose 180 degrees of windows afford views over the whole river system. A functional workspace with floor-to-ceiling bookshelves, master bedroom overlooking a deck with a hot tub and a view straight up into the mountains, and a luxurious his-and-hers bath and dressing rooms complete the ground floor; tucked downstairs are a media room and workout space. Comfortably furnished with locally handmade furniture, antler chandeliers, and Navajo rugs, the home's touchstone and greatest surprise (and every home should have one) is its powder room.

By some designer sleight-of-hand, the room manages to be charming rather than clichéd—truly an accomplishment considering that it's designed as the interior of an outhouse. Rough weathered barnwood paneling covers the walls and encases the outhouse-style commode; a tin pail complete with free-moving handle stands in for a sink. Rustic knickknacks complete the effect. Charm and originality carry the day in this fresh take on the Old West.

A two-level hillside aerie overlooks the confluence of the Upper South Fork River and Ishawooa Creek outside Cody, Wyoming. Built into the hillside, it is difficult to discern from a distance. The one-bedroom home and office features one large all-purpose gathering space. Little else is needed, given the expansive views.

A refurbished two-bedroom cabin built of two guest cabins from a historic dude ranch upriver is tucked out of sight in a grove of cotton-woods yet has spectacular views in three directions. In this setting, two bedrooms are all that's needed for a family of six.

ishawooa creek ranch

Just downstream and across two hay meadows, a riverside property draped along a mile of Shoshone River frontage corners at the confluence of Ishawooa Creek. Upstream, it's all heart-lifting upriver views of snow-capped peaks and open irrigated hay meadows. In the central section it's a cotton-wood-and-wildflower paradise for birds, interspersed with horse pasture. The downriver parcel is an untouched thicket, in the spring and early summer best left undisturbed due to the calving elk and, as a consequence, free-roaming grizzlies.

The previous owners had purchased two guest cabins from the Valley Ranch, a historic dude ranch four miles upriver. They relocated the cabins downstream, then joined them to create one livable structure. When an out-of-state family with young children bought the property, the husband and wife decided to upgrade the structure for year-round use but keep it as simple as possible to encourage the family to spend most of their time outdoors. Thus, there's just one small bedroom for the adults, a slightly larger bedroom for the four children, an updated and expanded kitchen opening to the original living/dining area, a small but efficient woodstove, a modern but rustic kitchen, and a porch wrapping around two sides, covered to offer protection from the squalls that blow down the valley.

Though the walls were insulated, the windows replaced, and the roof rebuilt and finished with cedar shakes, care was taken to retain the cabin's original effect. Its charm, after all, remained in the quirky details from its days as lodging for summer dudes: the original interior paneling, planks attacked with an adze in the 1940s to mimic hand-hewn beams; funky "closets" (actually cabinets hung with a section of pipe and outfitted with hooks made from coat hangers); an old-fashioned bottle opener mounted on the bathroom door sill; and a horseshoe framing the number 62 over the cabin's main door. All these details held sentimental value to the wife, who had worked as a wrangler on that very guest ranch throughout college.

Furnishings were kept minimal, a combination of turn-of-the-century "junk antiques," as the wife calls them, and furniture commissioned from the couple's artisan friends: a dining table by Ken Siggins, counter chairs by the late Mike Patrick of New West Furniture (each branded with one child's initial, to discourage squabbling), a corner table by Washington bent-willow artist Thome George, bunk beds by Cody builder Dave Strike, and the touchstone piece, a twisted juniper sconce by master rustic furniture maker Jim Covert.

Cowboy hats, antlers, and horse gear from Argentina are both functional and decorative in this simple western interior.

A sconce by acclaimed woodworker Jim Covert made from twisted juniper is the "touchstone" piece in this under-stated interior.

With minimal fencing and outbuildings (a tented cabin for guests, a couple of lean-tos for the horses, a campfire circle near river's edge, and one monumental hitching rail made from the trunk of a lodgepole pine), the property remains relatively wild for the wildlife passing through. Birds nest under the eaves, deer and moose wander through freely. And by the end of the first winter, a grizzly had left his calling card: a distinct paw print on the canvas of the tent cabin.

With less indoor area to which one can retreat, the children spend the entire day outdoors, grooming the horses and riding with their mom, checking the irrigating and fishing with their dad, collecting wildflowers and painting watercolors, and end-lessly reinforcing a dam where the irrigation runoff meets the river. In the evening, it's time around the campfire, listening to the river and admiring the sky as the sunset fades and the stars emerge. Through this simple approach to western living, less lit-erally becomes more.

the EJ

Across the river and just upstream from the Mariposa lies the EJ Ranch, originally homesteaded in 1931 by Norwegian settler Eli Jornberg. The home, a collection of cozy rooms with a remarkable low-ceilinged entry hall, glows with warmth from its narrow-diameter red-hued logs and wood trim, its rich patina reflecting its age. The owners, who moved to Wyoming from the Chesapeake Bay area in the mid 1980s, avidly embraced the rural Wyoming lifestyle: they ride, they hunt, they fish, they garden. They collect

An old trapper's cabin at the EJ Ranch typifies the patina of age found at the historic compound.

All the ranches of Cody's fabled Upper South Fork Valley share uplifting views and are surrounded by millions of acres of wilderness.

antique guns and like to fix things. The kitchen's old stainless-steel range and wicker baskets can handle a large crowd for cookouts and picnics, but nothing is more inviting than the dining room and kitchen, warmed by the oven and scented with baking cornbread, lit with candles and decorated with dried flower arrangements on a cold winter's night—a bit of heaven when you've just de-iced the horses' water in twenty-below weather.

In a home like this, rustic details give character: a leather pillow with a cowboy silhouette made by the couple's close friend, master leatherworker Lynda Covert; a birdhouse crafted from a cowboy boot, an old trapper's cabin hung with a flowering basket and antique creel, an antique truck with a gleaming stainless-steel grill and round headlights, and the original homesteader's brand inset into the front gate.

Despite the remoteness, sometimes loneliness in winter, the natural hazards, the harsh weather and relentless wind, says Melanie Lovelace, "We've loved living here. It's been the best nineteen years of our lives."

The new breed of contemporary western home expresses modernism while still respecting the land and recognizing the region's agricultural heritage. A thoughtfully designed home on a sensitively planned development sits lightly on the land and has a timeless appeal.

new prairie home

Early pioneers would have recognized the forms—if not the uber-clean materials and minimalist interiors—of the new breed of contemporary western home. These homes express modernism while still respecting the land and acknowledging the region's agricultural history. Sleek glass and steel structures perched high on a ridgetop make a dramatic statement, but thoughtful, quiet buildings make better neighbors.

Portland architect Doug Minarik studied and worked in Bozeman, Montana, for a decade. During that time he specialized in what he calls "human-scaled spaces," efficient homes that minimize resource use and energy waste and maximize natural benefits such as views and sunlight. In building large, he says, "There's a certain point where a home doesn't feel human anymore. You have to bring in big furniture to get it down to a human scale. But filling a home with extra stuff detracts from the volume and the views."

Minarik likes the luxury of building homes that are the result of what he calls a "thoughtful process." He describes this as projects that take a year or two to mature, and reflect a lot of dialogue with the owner. "They're not designing a home to sell in two or three years; they're designing a home to live in, one that will become [central to] their family."

While working with Comma-Q Architecture in Bozeman, Montana, the architect designed a home for a prairie-like parcel in Paradise Valley with a view of the Yellowstone River and a dramatic mountainscape backdrop. The client, Deb Kybartas, an L.A. entertainment assistant with teenage children, admits that her home on the range "was a dream fulfilled," she explains. "It didn't make sense to dive into a project such as this at this stage in my life, but the mountains are my first love and I thought,

Architect Doug Minarik specializes in what he calls "human-scaled spaces," efficient buildings that minimize resource use and energy waste and maximize natural benefits such as views and sunlight, both found in abundance in this Paradise Valley home.

Homeowner Deb Kybartas was looking for a "clean, simple, somewhat industrial-contemporary look, but with a pioneer spirit."

'What are you waiting for?' That drove me forward. I felt it was an important personal step in my life to take, and I have no regrets."

The client's wish was for "a clean, simple, somewhat industrial-contemporary look, with a pioneer spirit." As always, the first step, says the architect, was to walk the site with the owner, to get to know the land while getting to know the client—as well as the client's reactions to, perceptions of, and expectations of their new property.

Kybartas envisioned a barn-shaped structure, and she thought the master bedroom should be set apart from the central flow of the house to act as a true retreat. She wanted the structure for the main living space to maintain a lower profile, so as to "hug the earth." She also had the unusual but fixed notion of a sleeping porch. Minarik drew an initial sketch that envisioned a two-story barn-shaped building, a master suite over a garage, connected to the lower, ground-hugging structure. The connecting volume serves as both entryway and work area, its roof a logical place for a sleeping porch.

Clean lines, minimal color, and an open floor plan allow the ever-changing natural light to play a dynamic role in the interiors, and mean that there's less to distract the viewer from the changing colors in the landscape outside.

In this new prairie home, every aspect was considered before construction, whether it was the placement of windows, the angle of the sun, or the view from the bathtub.

"I tried hard to get the two-story volume to be an iconic barn-like structure," explains Minarik. "It serves as a marker in the landscape, while the other piece is really a windshelter. These small, simple forms are really connector pieces that create nice spaces between them. In small houses it's critical to enhance the outdoor spaces between the built forms. You get more overall value, and the outdoor space becomes just as special."

The home's exteriors—cedar siding and a metal roof—were kept as simple as possible, as were the interiors. "Usually people want to dump a lot of color into it," says Minarik, "but in this house, from morning to dusk the light is constantly changing; it's very dynamic. We kept it as simple and natural as possible. There's color only on the entry door and the kitchen cabinets, a light blue, and even that color is consistent. Because of that, you pay much more attention to the changing color in the landscape outside."

Clean minimal furnishings and natural materials make all the difference in a human-scaled home that feels big.

Clean, minimal furnishings and natural materials make all the difference in a human-scaled home that feels big. An entry hall that houses a workstation, a kitchen that's open to the dining and living areas yet defines its own space, a clever bedroom/bunkroom combo, and a master bedroom retreat, only slightly removed yet away from it all. . . . These are the elements of one successful home on the range.

Minarik credits the project's success, and the owner's happiness in her new home, with their careful approach to design. "We took our time," he says. "We worked at a very comfortable pace, over three years. I worked a lot with hand sketches and little vignettes of kitchen views and many iterations so Deb would get a sense of how it would play out. We played with Google Earth and drew lines to primary views. We moved a series of windows up a foot and a half to create carefully placed vignettes and apertures.

A clever workstation in the entry hall is a good use of otherwise wasted space. Says the owner, "I wanted it clean and simple, even though I love warm and cozy. I wanted to come in and not feel burdened by stuff."

We even rotated the house five degrees when excavating for the short-range and long-range views. Now every moment you walk through the house reveals different bits of the landscape. We really paid attention the whole way through."

Designing carefully and allowing time for the plans to gestate are important, but as Kybartas points out, "When creating a house of this nature it's important to let go of micromanaging the details in order to enjoy the process. Of course, it's the guidance of a gifted architect and highly skilled contractor that made that possible. They both really were able to grasp what I was trying to accomplish."

She says pairing with the right architect—and then trusting him to realize one's vision—is crucial. Says Doug Minarik. "In Montana and Wyoming, so many homes are second homes. As an architect you hope that it's personal enough—and that it's about the person as well as the site."

The ranch house is ubiquitous on the residential side streets of towns throughout the West, and on ranches as well. This example, tucked into a sloping hillside, is protected from the wind yet still has far-reaching views and lots of sunlight.

1950s
ranch house
redux

Turn off the main street of any medium sized town in the
mountain west—Thermopolis or Sheridan, Wyoming; Hamilton
or Red Lodge, Montana; Rexburg or Hailey, Idaho—and drive
the side streets. You'll find the usual mixture of styles, from
stucco to Arts & Crafts-influenced bungalows with porches.
But mostly you'll find ranch houses: simple, low-slung, one-
story homes of wood or brick, their garages typically facing
the street, their concrete or stone paths leading up to the front
door. Out of sight but surely present is a sliding glass door to
the ubiquitous patio or deck behind the house, in keeping
with the indoor-outdoor lifestyle glorified during southern
California's postwar decades.

The owners, a native Montanan and an interior designer from New York, were charmed by the home's sense of family history as a three-generation family cattle ranch. They strived to re-create this feeling by honoring what was there. For instance, says the wife, "The 1950s sofa is inconsistent and not western, but we honored the history of the house. I try to find objects that speak to each other."

First finding expression in the 1920s and 1930s, and so named as taking its cue from early Californian "ranchos," the ranch house was popularized by architects across the country in the 1940s, '50s, and '60s. It became the most widespread American home style during that time. The ranch home was a modern yet modest and practical approach to a newly pressing residential need: that of a single family of busy individuals pursuing an informal, modern, and self-sufficient (i.e., servant-less) lifestyle. Its form was well adapted to the mountain West, where crowding is not an issue but high winds are. A low-profile structure on a spacious lot seemed a good fit for many of these mountain towns, as well as a practical approach for ranch owners. (Thus many "ranch homes" literally are that.)

"When we came in the first time there was a portrait of the owner's great-grandfather in the corner," recalls the owner. "This is not a family portrait but it captures exactly the spirit of the man who's been watching over this living room for ages. It's also a funny little reminder of the eastern man in his western living room."

Excluding the glamorous designs of California architect Cliff May, who designed ten thousand original structures and published designs for another eighteen thousand houses throughout the country—the ranch home was not a fashion statement as much as a lifestyle statement. It was utilitarian, with few decorative elements; it was designed for the convenience breakthroughs of the '40s as well as a newly informal lifestyle which mandated indoor public spaces that flowed into one another and easy access to the outdoors.

The ranch home's lack of glamour, dearth of drama, and absence of rustic regional elements mean that this style has never been the first choice in western architecture for those seeking a western retreat or mountain home. Somehow it can be difficult to feel you've gotten away from it all when your home resembles a quarter of the homes in suburban America. But a classic ranch home on a hillside near the Beartooth Mountains near the Wyoming/Montana border proves that the western home is where the heart is, and that if you work with the elements you're given the result can be uniquely charming—and very western indeed.

The owners, a cattle rancher born and raised in Montana and his wife, an interior design professional who built her career in New York, say that unlike most ranch houses, theirs was not built for its site. Rather, an argument that escalated to a proper falling-out resulted in a home being chain-sawed in half; half stayed put on its site, the other half was dragged up the hill and repositioned. With its glorious flowering trees and its early-era stone root cellar built into the hillside behind the house, one would never suspect that the house wasn't site-specific in its design. Elevated by several hundred feet off a quiet country road of twists and turns, the home is snugly tucked into the landscape while boasting far-reaching views and much sunlight.

The home's exterior is pleasingly simple: two horizontal volumes, one double height, with a brick chimney between them; wood siding painted brown; and a long covered porch, perfect for outdoor dining. Its interiors, though, seem to tell a story.

When they first saw the house, recalls the owner, they were immediately charmed, despite the home's obvious lack of drama. "One of the reasons we were able to work with it so well was that we had the benefit of seeing it when the previous owner was still living in it, with all its layers of history," explains the designer. "If we had seen it after they moved their things out it would have looked like a carcass of the 1940s. But their [belongings] made the house feel very relevant and current, each decade leaving its mark."

Nothing conveys a sense of history more convincingly than an old root cellar, still in use today.

She sought to re-create that feeling, not of a home that had been "decorated," but of a home filled with family mementos, ranch-life artifacts, and an eclectic mix of period furniture and furnishings. "When we went back and furnished it," she recalls, "we used furniture from mid-century to current; we had some heirloom pieces, western antiques and European antiques as well."

The result is a confident mixing of styles that's a tribute to the owners' willingness to work with an existing slate rather than ripping out the old to create a blank new one. In the living room, there's a 1950s upholstered couch with narrow wooden legs, wicker saucer chairs, and an old wood desk on turned legs; a dark carved mirror hangs above it. A phonograph cabinet with built-in speakers still boasts a working turntable under a sliding top; this was a uniquely fitting housewarming gift from the husband's parents.

The mildly midcentury modern details pair with old oil paintings of western wilderness scenes, a wood-topped table on an antler base, two vintage lighting fixtures suspended from the ceiling, three 1940s ranch-home-style lantern-shaped brass lamps with green shades, and a buffalo hide thrown across the floor. A green leather chair shares one end of the room with a card table and three velvet-upholstered chairs. A portrait suggesting someone's grandfather presides over late-night poker games.

Although a beamed ceiling and river-rock fireplace are not typical of ranch-style homes, in this case they are authentic. "The fireplace was in the original drawing but was probably rebuilt after the house was chain-sawed in two and this half was dragged up the hill," explains the owner. "The beams were oak scraped with a steel brush, which gives interior structure. It was so cool we decided to leave it. All the elements were there; we left it exactly how it was and just added furniture, rugs, lamps, and lighting."

"I try to find the feeling of the house," says the designer. "I try to think of each room as a person; I invent a story about them in my head and edit out anything that doesn't belong. I had a story in my head about who lived there, and it wasn't us."

The home's three bedrooms, two baths, living room, kitchen, and dining room all benefit from what the designer calls "layering," which she achieves through a variety of means, starting with color.

For example, she explains, "When we did the kitchen, we said, 'Let's renovate to 1920 instead of 2006.' The kitchen had been renovated, but instead of designing a new kitchen we found the original plans for the house. We went with a cabinet design that we could see from the drawings; we wanted that old-fashioned hygienic feeling. Each wall is a slightly different color so that it doesn't feel like it was all done yesterday. It feels like different layers of paint that don't match up perfectly."

Simplicity was important in this space. "There are barely any appliances. There's no backsplash, no tilework. There's a seat that lifts and underneath that is a laundry chute into the basement. There's a little desk with a household phone. It has a painted wood floor. We wanted to keep it as ranch-y as possible." Now, she says, "The kitchen has become a gathering place."

Perhaps the most unique room in the home is the Three Bears room, an Austrian-inspired room that takes its cue from the home's placement "up on a hill, surrounded by a ring of pine trees." The wall color is a deep green, an unusual choice for a bedroom that doesn't have windows to the exterior. "We felt it was going to be hopelessly dark," the designer explains, "so instead of trying to make it light we turned it into a bear's den with the dark green walls. It's a nice contrast to the kitchen. Again, it's about working with what you have and going with the flow. If it's a dark room," she adds, "it's a dark room."

The home's easy simplicity, unique details, and period charm combine to create a feeling of true refuge. "This house doesn't only look like a period house; it sounds like one, too," says the owner. "We put in antique phones so that when someone calls

When the designer contemplated the kitchen, she suggested to her husband that they renovate to 1920 rather than 2006. They followed the original house plans for the kitchen and designed cabinets accordingly. White paint colors were deliberately mis-matched to con-vey a feeling of the room's layers of history. The lighting fixtures, which can be raised and low-ered, came out of an old bakery.

The Austrian-inspired Three Bears Room has an unusual feature: it has no windows to the outdoors. Rather than trying to make it light and bright, the designer opted to turn it into a bear's den. She clustered European-style mounts on the wall, assembled heritage-feel antiques, and painted the walls a deep, cozy green.

there's a 1940s phone ringing. There's no TV and no internet, so it's a great place to relax."

Clearly the success of the house lies in honoring the structure's history and highlighting what's interesting and unique rather than seeking transformation. "It's about the house and the house's history," asserts the designer. "It's not about the owners coming in and leaving their stamp; the concept is of preserving things as a ruin. It's not an expression of our style, but an homage to this house and its history as a family cattle ranch."

"The concept is of preserving things as a ruin. It's not an expression of our style, but an homage to this house and its history as a family cattle ranch."

The most effective
way to limit a
building's impact
on the surrounding
wildness is to build
minimally, naturally,
and off the grid.

off the western grid

It's the quintessential conundrum for people who are passionate about a pristine place, whether that place is virgin wilderness in the Rockies or a traditional village in an exotic location: how does one indulge this passion without contributing to the degradation of the very essence of the experience?

The Rocky Mountains' special places, although seemingly limitless, are slowly being chipped away, encroached upon, and eroded. As more people move to the mountain West in pursuit of their western dream, and increasing numbers of visitors embrace the active outdoor lifestyle, the consequent effects—from increased traffic to compromised streambeds to stressed wildlife to snowmobile exhaust in Yellowstone National Park—are compounded. A property owner may want to build as the pioneers did, low and modest, but he still has infrastructure needs to consider. The Currier & Ives effect of a remote cabin on the edge of the wilderness is definitely undermined by its access road, power lines, telephone wires, and septic system. Today, living lightly on the land by definition means considering alternative technologies to minimize impacts and to avoid disrupting natural habitat as much as possible.

Montana architect Jonathan Foote has achieved an international reputation as someone who thinks in a new way about old materials. Reclaimed materials have a patina of age and use that speak to him. But using old materials to build an oversized mansion defeats the purpose, from his point of view. All architecture should be site-specific, and, he feels, should be a process that evolves naturally and sensitively when one's intuition is engaged.

"The selection of a place to build is a first indicator that a client is connected to the site," Foote explains. "They've picked it for an emotional reason. I always start there with a client. I say, 'What do you like?' and very often they say, 'I don't know.' Which is good because if you intellectualize it, it's weakened." After all, he adds, "When you pitch your camp after a long ride into the mountains, you pick a place that feels good to you."

When Foote first met the client who would become a long-time collaborator as well as close friend and travel companion, he didn't know much about him other than the man was a native Montanan whose first ranch purchase represented a sort of homecoming after a long professional life in New York. The original site the client showed Foote was breathtaking. An almost inaccessible ranch surrounded by national forest and on the edge of the precipitous Clark's Fork Canyon, it featured spectacular views west into the high peaks of Yellowstone National Park. Over the course of the next couple of years they created multiple structures in rustic materials; the ultimate result was a cluster of classic dwellings, outbuildings, and barns dramatically perched on a high plateau.

"Finding the right place is the key to starting a relationship in the process of building a house," Foote explains. "You build up from that point; it grows on its own. You don't try to force it, or manipulate it. You use it, and enjoy the choreography of getting into the site. Then you continue the choreography as you go into

Layers of wood and timeless materials convey a sense of history and authenticity even in a new structure.

Architect Jonathan Foote, a proponent of regionally appropriate site-specific architecture, says that interiors in remote locations need to be comfortable and feel secure. After all, he points out, "When you go out, there might be a grizzly bear, or a mountain lion, or a gale blowing."

the interiors, with the views, the sound of the stream, or the whistle of the wind in the pines. That all becomes part of the dance, and the form comes out of all those sensations. It's not a formal exercise; it's a purely intuitive process. I tell clients, 'We're not building a house yet. We're selecting the instruments that are going to play in the orchestra.'"

In the case of the uber-dramatic setting above the canyon, he recalls, "There were several buildings in one state or another of useability. We had to [design] in a very overpowering landscape, with tubas and trumpets and all kinds of electrified musical instruments. It's easy for the buildings to lie quietly even though they're exposed, because the scenery is so extraordinary."

Several years later, the client had expanded his cattle operation and wanted to show Foote another property he'd purchased. The large parcel of land—open hills, aspens and forests, with live water, on the edge of true wilderness—was untouched. It was also

In these quiet,
frontier-like
interiors, nothing
is jarringly modern
or out of place.

barely accessible. "He wanted to keep it small-scale, and he wanted to keep it as self-sufficient as possible," Foote explains. "The land seemed to me [to suggest a] pretty natural organization of buildings; they would look and feel as though this whole thing was snugged down in there, with a great deal of land around it, and a great deal of sky above it, and the mountains."

While exterior design was critical in such a pristine site, Foote explains, the interiors were also extremely important. "It had to be a comfortable complex: you come in and sit by the fire and pour yourself a drink and you're secure. Because when you go out there might be a grizzly bear, or a mountain lion, or a gale blowing."

But before even contemplating the structures, let alone the interiors, one thing was abundantly clear, says the architect. "Self sufficiency was demanded by the distance it was from a telephone and a power line." Rather than stringing wires across the landscape, they installed solar panels and a wind generator to meet the buildings' energy needs. They captured a spring to create a

tranquil pond and positioned a hot tub to overlook it. The buildings, grouped in a cluster on a gently sloping grade, linked by paths, and surrounded by a buck-and-rail fence, consist of a two-bedroom main lodge with a tiny kitchen open to the living room; a dining table visually separates the spaces on one end, while a fireplace anchors the other. Two sleeping cabins nestled among some aspens beside the placid surface of the pond accommodate several more guests. A utility building houses all the instruments and technology for the power systems—as well as a canoe for the pond, and outdoor gear for exploring the surrounding backcountry.

The camplike red-roofed complex has a timeless, weathered look; its only nod to modernity is its cluster of pole-mounted solar panels, positioned a distance from the buildings up a steep hill to best capture any available sunlight. A rustic fence protects the panels from ever-curious bears, or the bull elk in need of a scratching post when his antlers are ready to drop.

A textured buck-and-rail fence surrounding shiny high-tech solar panels. . . . It may seem a mixing of metaphors, but these are the elements of a truly modern homestead—off-the-grid, western-style.

The modern homestead is epitomized by the contrast between rustic and high-tech: antique logs and shiny solar panels surrounded by a buck-and-rail fence.

A three-building, three-year project almost entirely driven by art features an agricultural form for the studio and office and a Shaker-inspired barn. "This valley is essentially a working valley," says artist Karen Carson, who designed the buildings with local architects. "I thought, why not keep the working vernacular that's in the valley?"

new western farmhouse

Some building projects are about architecture; some are about interiors. Some are driven by function, some by limitations of the site, or realities of the weather, or restrictions of the building codes. And some are driven by art. Some projects are even built around art: in such projects, buildings are showcases, buildings become frames.

Karen Carson is a professional painter, born and raised on the west coast. She had spent her adult life in New York City and southern California living in gritty lofts rather than comfortable houses, in a world dominated by art and intellect rather than wildlife and scenery. George Wanless was an Idaho rancher who over the course of many years had built an important and decidedly surprising collection of modernist western art at the Nora Eccles Harrison Museum at Utah State University. They met when Wanless purchased a painting of Carson's for the museum; their life together has been guided by art ever since.

"We live with art everywhere," says Karen Carson. "It's not about investment; buying on speculation is anathema to us. It's about having things around you that please you every time you look at them. It's about 'the life of the eyes.'"

Bringing an artist's eye, and an art-collector's eye, to a multi-structure project in small-town Montana created a special set of circumstances: three structures, built in three stages, with three different architects, over three years. The structures were designed to the artist's vision; the specifications were handled by the architects; and the ultimate realization was accomplished by one very competent local contractor, Terry Talkington.

"We live with art everywhere. It's not about investment; it's about having things around you that please you every time you look at them. It's about 'the life of the eyes.'"

Since art drove the project, the studio was built first while the couple lived in a trailer on the property. Carson knew the height the walls needed to be and had an idea for a barn-shaped structure with two cupolas; she knew she needed a massive rolling door on one side of the building through which she could move her largest canvasses. The building's ultimate mass was determined from those criteria. An entry with a small porch opens to a room with stairs leading up to Wanless' office. A screened porch runs the length of the building on one side, providing an airy place for Carson to do any sawing, drilling, and sanding. It's also "the relaxing space," she says. "I sit out there and read."

The home, owned by an artist and an art curator, was built to house art and is a collection of collections, from primitive found art and folk art lamps to carved wood-and-tile furniture from India. On the walls hang etchings, drawings, photographs, and oil paintings, mostly chronicling the mountain West.

The remainder of the structure is one soaring open space for art, a large, well-lit painting studio with plenty of natural light. It was there Carson started work on her first Montana paintings, large works on silk that became the subject of a one-woman show at the Pomona College Museum of Art. Clearly Carson has been moved by the dramas of nature she's experienced since living in Montana. She chose to tackle a dynamic and edgy subject: not charismatic wildlife or monumental scenery, but forest fires. In an attempt to convey the awesome power of nature, some of the fire paintings are twenty-four feet in length. "Up here, the skies are either full of clouds or full of flames," she explains of her subject matter. "The paintings had to be big because I wanted them to approximate some level of fury."

*　　　　*　　　　*

The studio completed, the garage, its design based on a Shaker barn, was next, built big enough for cars as well as farm equipment. Lastly, the couple turned to the house. Although from a

An intimately scaled workstation gives way to the soaring ceiling of the studio, whose doors had to be tall enough to roll Carson's largest canvases through.

distance it looks like a collection of buildings—or one farm building added onto in different directions over the decades—the home is basically a U-shaped building built around a wind-sheltered entry area of green lawn and stone pavers with a wraparound porch. The house has light-filled rooms; unusual features such as doily-shaped windows; a small square room that mimics a European-style library with windows on three sides and an oculus-like cupola; and an astounding array of color combinations. More than one hundred colors were used in the painting of the house, all to Carson's specifications.

The buildings' exteriors are a medley of colors—terra-cotta, yellow, gray, maroon, blue—that change according to the viewer's orientation. The visual experience has been considered from every angle. For instance, says Carson, "All the eaves as you look up anywhere are painted blue so you have the feeling that the sky's coming down through the roof."

Indoors, she continues, "I like framing devices, so there's a lot of outlining going on." In the living room, three tiers of moldings

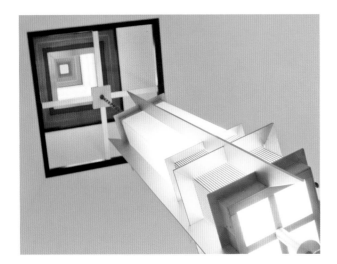

around square windows placed high up off the floor are each painted a different shade of blue "to create a kind of telescoping of the blue sky." In the kitchen, the beams are painted three colors, with a fourth a stripe that wraps around the ceiling. For the floor of the entry hall, Carson selected eighteen shades of old-fashioned linoleum tile—orange, wine, sage, browns, tans—and requested one-inch-by-one-inch color samples of each. "I just sat down and moved them around until I got the pattern I wanted."

Carson is particularly conscious of the way in which color affects mood, and she uses it to effect. "In each room I used color to try to create a sensation. The living room is keyed down; it's more urban, with blacks, blues, grays, and sage green. It's a really quiet room. The kitchen is a high-energy room." The guest room, a place of refuge, is taupe. "A lot of people don't notice the color they're in," adds Carson, "but they feel it."

The dining room is the only room in the house that "is meant to be part of the landscape," says Carson. "It's made like a hop silo. The colors mimic the colors in the field, and the ceiling is blue so it feels like sky. It's the one room in the house that I wanted to open up to the environment." As for the rest of the house, she adds, "If you're drenched in nature all day—with the sun and blue sky and browns—you want the inside to be a contrast to the outside."

As an artist, Carson used color liberally and to careful effect throughout the house. "In each room I used color to try to create a sensation." More than one hundred colors were used throughout the house, all to Carson's specifications.

The home boasts an unusual and varied museum-quality collection of collections. Scattered throughout the house are the couple's accumulated antique and folk-art lamps; "oddball primitive found art," such as collages and needlework; and carved-wood-and-tile furniture from India. In the kitchen is a collection of painted water glasses, and another of mixing bowls from the 1950s. There is yet another of antique salt-and-pepper shakers, approximately two hundred sets on display in two custom-made cabinets, from an ink bottle with spilled ink to a bucking bronco with the cowboy who's been bucked off. "We're junk-store fiends. We started collecting those on our first date." Now, admits Carson, "The house is just littered with minor collections."

But it's the fine art throughout the house that commands center stage. Paintings, etchings, photographs, and drawings hang on every wall, almost all chronicling the mountain West. Most fall into the modernist movement. "The art comes out of cubism and abstract expressionism and follows the development of modern art

in the West," explains Carson. "George is a trained historian who's good at researching and chasing things down. He's collected a lot of great artists that haven't quite gotten the attention. He's kind of a visionary."

That shared vision has created a home that speaks to the region's agricultural heritage—and the nearby red-and-white farm buildings of a neighbor's ranch—yet it is truly unique. It's an original statement about immersion in art. There, art is not merely decorative, but all-encompassing. It's a lifestyle and a passion, and an honest expression of western style.

The roomy, well-lit farm kitchen showcases more of the couple's collections, such as hand-painted water glasses, 1950s mixing bowls, and two hundred sets of salt and pepper shakers. Carson designed all the bookcases, beams, shelving, counters and moldings. "I did little drawings trying to work out proportions and design. I had a pile of maybe three hundred sketches. I have a completely new respect for architects and designers. Theirs is a hard job."

A multiple-dwelling project set within a vast working cattle ranch had as its starting point the river system and natural landscape. First addressed was land restoration. Buildings came later. The results were remarkable, says the owner, a former board member of Trout Unlimited. "The previous owner had straightened the river. We put the structure back into it, with interesting twists and turns. I've been asked how long it takes for the trout to find these pools. The answer is five minutes."

reclaimed
ranch

The American West is characterized by its mountains—and also by the distances between them. As anyone who has ever driven the rural highways of the northern Rockies knows, the extreme distances between towns require stocking up on fuel, water, and road food before continuing on. "Next services, 85 miles" is not an uncommon sight. In wintertime, most natives store sleeping bags and flares in their trunks, just in case. On those lonely stretches of highway, the very emptiness is thrilling—although that doesn't mean drivers don't addictively read billboards, or aren't deeply grateful when they find a radio station amidst all the static. In this context, the sight of an antelope bounding across open sagebrush hills can be simply exhilarating.

But there's a melancholy, too, in all that emptiness: in the interstate highway exits that seemingly lead nowhere; in the wooden signs for remote ranches whose residents have no neighbors; in the "for sale" signs on the 1940s-era hot springs "resorts" by the side of the highway. But more than anything it is in the abandoned cabins, barns, and schoolhouses that punctuate the mountain West. For every magnificent new trophy home built in an upscale resort town, for every new subdivision that sprouts up outside a growing population center, somewhere in the water-deprived fastness there's a corresponding homestead-era log or stone structure, its roof collapsed, slowly disintegrating into the soil. Each represents an individual family story. Together, they tell the history of the settlement of the West, at a time when "Go West, young man," was a call heard by every ambitious young man (and some women) with a strong back and the will to take his chances on building a better life.

These structures speak to Montanan Tom Norquist, who himself went west as a young man from Minnesota. His longtime interest in historic preservation found fertile ground in the homestead West, a place where abandoned dwellings are plentiful and sensitive landowners can be found who value the beauty and history of century-old structures. He has spent close to three decades giving

Denver designer Patsy Psaledakis says of the project, made from reclaimed cabins by local builder-craftsman Tom Norquist: "It's all about nature and the environment and the land. Both of the owners are about preserving the land as it is. They want to live amid it, not make a statement. It's more personal and intimate this way, and it's incredibly special."

The heart of the main lodge was a large log barn salvaged in Montana's Paradise Valley; the Dutch lap siding was made of reclaimed material found in Judith Gap. Separate sleeping cabins force the owners and their guests out into the elements.

old logs a second chance, simultaneously preserving the heritage of the West while creating beautiful, unique homes. "I really enjoy working with old logs," says Norquist. "I know where they came from, and I love to learn about the homesteaders who had their dreams and their heartbreaks in those buildings. Those buildings," he adds, "have a soul."

When asked to visit the site of a ranch on Big Timber Creek, Norquist drove across miles of open cattle pasture belonging to one of the largest and oldest ranches in Sweet Grass County, and he was surprised when the dirt road deposited him down in a hollow, a sweet spot protected from the wind at the curve of the river.

The property owner had a longtime history in Montana ranching and a passion for nature; he also had a global perspective, having lived abroad and having traveled the world writing and shooting documentaries. He was very matter-of-fact about the site. "It was a total, absolute mess," he recalls. "But it was so private, it had a great view of the Crazy Mountains, and it had the river."

At the time a Board member of Trout Unlimited, the owner's first priority was to restore the river to its natural course and to recreate the wetland that had existed prior to the previous owner's building of roads, digging of ponds, and diverting of the river. For this he brought in fishery and stream-restoration experts, who worked in conjunction with the federal and state governments. "We knew we had a huge project on our hands," he explains, "but we were committed to getting the river and water systems right. The pond leaked two hundred gallons a minute, so we got rid of that. We put in eighteen acres of wetlands and converted agricultural water rights to wetlands water rights. The local farmers thought we were nuts."

Soon, though, the river had slowed to its natural current, the specimen trees on the property, ancient silver poplars, were flourishing, and wildlife was thriving in the restored environment. "We had a mountain lion not twenty feet from the lodge," says the owner, "and the bears come down for chokecherries every August. We have partridge, turkeys, golden eagles. We've heard wolves, and we hear coyotes every night. We have a wonderful fishery. Every year we have the wetlands and bird life monitored, and every year we gain about four new species. The force of nature has been absolutely staggering."

Habitation was next, with the barn preceding the lodgings. "We had all these barns that were falling down and falling apart," recalls the owner. "[Local builder] Keith Green took an old

In the main lodge, a great room furnished with artifacts collected during the husband's years in Africa and art collected during the wife's long international art-world career connects to a kitchen, mud room, and dining room, while an open gallery with a rustic railing encircles the room above. Local stonemason John Baker collected all the rocks for the fireplace out of the creek and along the hillside above the house.

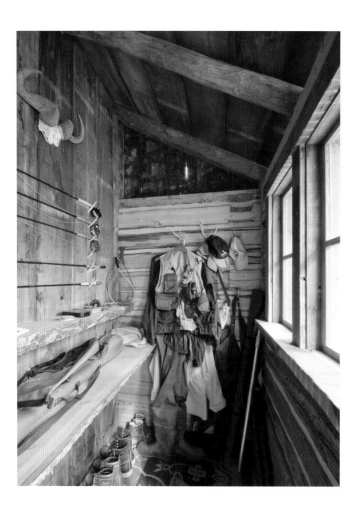

A separate fly-tying shack is a fisherman's dream, with plenty of room for waders, rods, reels, and boots.

bunkhouse, skidded it over, and built the barn around it; he also built the shop and the shed. We heard about Tom Norquist; there was a homesteader cabin that was falling down that was about one hundred years old. It had been used as a chicken house. Tom took it down, numbered the logs, power washed it, and restacked it by the river. Then he drove us up into Paradise Valley where there was a barn and a granary for sale. They needed a lot of love, but the wood was in great shape. That barn became the heart and the life of our main lodge."

The largest of the buildings, the barn became the two-story living room. Bozeman architect Graham Goff used the existing openings to design the kitchen, dining room, mud room, and pantry. Tucked downstairs are the guest room, office, and laundry.

The living room, filled with fascinating artifacts, interesting books, and spectacular art gathered by the owner and his wife, a longtime art-world professional at Sotheby's, has an open gallery at its top for overflow sleeping. The heart of the home is its stone fireplace constructed by a local stonemason from rocks collected on the property.

The sleeping cabin for the owners and their daughter is a simple structure with two bedrooms, fireplace, bath, and small sitting room; its generous deck overlooks the river. A nearby guest cabin is an exercise in compact coziness, with its brass beds, small ladder-accessed loft, and wood-burning stove. Completing the camplike feel are the barn, with its tidy corral tucked among the trees, the washhouse, and a fishing cabin sited next to a tranquil pond surrounded by cattails.

A charming guest cabin has just what one needs for a good night's sleep: a comfortable bed, a good reading light, and a wood stove. A cleverly designed closet has a tiny built-in book-shelf and a flat top, making room for vintage finds and a pair of cowboy-and-Indian book-ends by artist Buckeye Blake.

"The project was two or three years in the making, but we were very deliberate about how we went about it," says the ranch owner. "We just really took our time. Tom is an old-fashioned craftsman; he only works with two or three guys, and nothing is store bought. We're so committed to his work that we have the remains of another building in stacks. He came to us and said that the first ranch in Wisdom, Montana, was available. It's all square cut inside, and round cut on the outside. We don't know what we'll do with it, but it's there."

Norquist, for his part, finds each project a fascinating exercise in preservation. He resurrects a piece of history while positioning it to become part of a client's family story. "To me, working with old logs is way more satisfying than new con-struction," says Norquist. "And it's a super creative process. All we have is a basic blueprint. We use old materials, like twisted juniper and whatever else happens to be there. The creative process just happens as the project unfolds. The materials have an integrity. My job is to let that come out. These logs are holding an energy within them. It's not about me making a statement; it's, 'Get out of the way and let the materials speak for themselves.'"

"The materials have an integrity.

My job is to let that come out.

It's not about me making a

statement; it's, 'Get out of

the way and let the materials

speak for themselves.'"

Historic preservation in the West serves dual purposes. It maintains a region's history as an important link to the past. It's also a key component of the sustainability puzzle. As Richard Moe, Director of the National Trust for Historic Preservation, puts it, "When you strip away the rhetoric, preservation is simply having the good sense to hold onto things that are well designed, that link us with our past in a meaningful way, and that have plenty of good use left in them."

"The idea of the bedroom and guesthouse cabins," says builder Tom Norquist, "was that you could open the doors and windows and hear the roar of the river all through the night."

Montana Architect Larry Pearson is known for his expressive rustic designs, but for his own Bozeman home he renovated a mid-century house designed by MSU Dean of Architecture Oswald Berg, Jr. In updating the home and building a barn and combined guesthouse/greenhouse, Pearson drew on his early training during his formative years exploring solar technology and green design in California.

eco home
on the range

Mid-century modern seems neither historic nor western when compared to century-old structures such as a homesteader's cabin, a stone granary, or the Old Faithful Inn. But even mid-century design takes on the aura of history after the passage of six decades. And it is western when it's intelligently designed, celebrates local materials, employs recyclables in its construction and décor, and is fully integrated into and sensitive to its site. Taking a step further—creating a sustainably designed structure with minimum energy needs in an extreme climate—truly honors the West. It puts the environment first and is a bold example of the self-reliance on which westerners made their reputation.

Bozeman architect Larry Pearson had built his career designing spectacular handcrafted log and stone homes in some of the most beautiful parts of the American West. For his own home, however, he had purchased an architecturally significant house in need of updating set on a very special piece of property: a four and a half-acre lot within a two thousand–acre conservation-eased ranch on the edge of one of Montana's most dynamic towns. Just minutes from the Pearson Design Group's office, it also offered quick access to the skiing, hiking, and kayaking that had first drawn Pearson to Montana back in 1988.

The house, designed by Oswald Berg, Jr., when Dean of Architecture at Montana State University, was built in 1957. Pearson acquired the property, still in its original state, when he was a bachelor. Originally there had been a main house, a garage, and a small shed, "quaint and quirky," recalls Pearson Design Group interior designer Rain Turrell.

Marriage and children meant an update was inevitable. Clearly this property was never going to be a rustic showplace. And Pearson, a native Californian, had spent the early part of his career in the 1970s exploring the possibilities of solar power in Santa Cruz. He felt compelled to honor the original designer's vision; he also had a chance to experiment with ideas he'd been thinking about for years. The project became an intellectual puzzle, Pearson recalls. "The question was, 'How do you do something sensitively, with energy efficiency in mind? How do you create a four-building complex that is off the grid, or zero-grid, and essentially sustainable?' I found myself going back to what I had been doing twenty-five years ago, when I was using passive solar energy in home design."

Pearson's sensitive update of the home, and construction of barn, combined guest house/greenhouse, and garden—"reflects

A track system for transparent, gauzy materials was designed by Pearson Design Group's Interior Designer Rain Turrell to flow over and around the home's steel column. "It creates a screen of fabric against the translucency of the windows and floating roof," says Pearson. "It's all about me wanting to be outside."

A locally quarried boulder was chosen for the hearth, which floats atop a concrete base. The chairs were designed by Sergio Rodriguez, a Brazilian designer of the 1960s.

the same values of modern 1959 architecture carried forward," he asserts. "The guest house, barn, and shop building are designed to read like a modern compound, with vertical butted whitewashed planks, no eaves, intersecting horizontal metal awnings, and breezeway connections detailed in steel. The roofs are of rusting corrugated steel." The result is a compound of buildings that are original and modern yet speak to the region's heritage while tying to the landscape.

"I grew up in an Eichler home in San Francisco," Pearson explains. "To me, this carries on those Eichler values." The architect asked himself, "What is the evolution of Eichler, as far as family values? What is the evolution of the homestead or the farm—because this is a property with red barns in the landscape? So I put together a distillation of a western barn motif with west coast Eichler influences. That was my thinking on the evolution of what was the New Utopia. In California it's pretty easy; with the exception of fog and wind, temperatures are pretty moderate. In

A mid-century modern cabinet, Hawaiiana lithographs by John Kelly, and a Chagall print ("my only real piece of art," says Pearson) set nicely against mahogany walls. A handwaxed concrete floor is set with black pebbles at the entryway.

Montana you need to be much more careful. Outdoor living needs to be south-facing, and buildings need to be hunkered down for wind protection. Original trees need to be set to the west or southwest to break the wind. You need to focus on what it means to be outdoors at different times of the day." For instance, he asks, "How do you create a space that's comfortable for entertaining in the early evening, which is when most people entertain?"

Pearson pondered these questions at length, designing as he worked through the process. The result is a main house, built of glass, steel, concrete, and wood beams, that is serene without being spare, light-filled without being overscaled, and modern without being ascetic. "Contemporary can be severe, uncomfortable," says Pearson. "Most of us want a softer environment. But how do you introduce softness? A true modern house on a midwinter day can be harsh. We used layers of curtains that fuse light without glare. That's one of the problems with bright southern light. The use of transparent fabric can make it much more livable."

Because the Pearsons cook out-doors frequently, they decided they could keep the kitchen small and functional. Bamboo cabinetry, an absolute granite backsplash, and steel and black walnut shelves set the tone, while reproduction vintage stools lend an industrial look.

Floor-to-ceiling glass, large pivoting glass doors, an eclectic mix of midcentury modern furniture, open shelving in the compact kitchen, and concrete floors all speak to a clean, contemporary aesthetic. Radiant heat, passive solar considerations, and very tight fittings ensure that the glass house is comfortable even in the most severe temperatures.

The remainder of the compound is equally thoughtful. The barn houses two sustainable businesses run by Pearson's wife, Jennifer. She raises alpacas for wool and has launched an alpaca fiber business. And her solar-powered company, Glass Roots, hand-manufactures beautiful art tiles for bath and kitchen installations made from recycled bottles.

The guesthouse, attached to a greenhouse, is a study in compact design. The bed is a sofa with an ottoman; the two can be pushed together to make a queen bed.

But it is in the guest house that Pearson's ideas reach full flower. "It was originally going to be a greenhouse, then I decided to make it a 'green house,' meaning the greenhouse would heat the guesthouse. I was also exploring the idea of what can be done for $80,000 that an individual or couple could live in. For me it's an expression of simplicity and energy efficiency, but it also delivers something at a real price point."

The diminutive cottage-like structure has a sleeping area, a small kitchen with table and chairs, and large doors that open wide to the outdoors. An attached steel greenhouse is covered with custom steel shingles, all slowly rusting. From placement to interiors, every aspect of the structure was considered. For instance, Pearson explains. "We dropped the building two and a half feet into the ground so that it's low on the landscape. But how do you

The greenhouse is accessible from both doors in this tiny cottage. The doors open up completely for a true indoor-outdoor experience—and direct access to the extensive flowerbeds and organic garden.

get light into the house to minimize the need for electric light? It's held back from the tree line to get the arc of the sun even on winter days; it gets light from morning to afternoon."

A series of raised beds set into the garden ensure a long growing season at high altitude and plentiful harvest meals enjoyed al fresco. The Pearsons can be comfortable even in the evening thanks to carefully sited outdoor entertaining spaces with concrete walls and steel panels that absorb heat during the day and radiate it back out in the evening. Lest they mistake Bozeman for Santa Cruz, however, grazing cattle serve as a reminder of the ranch country they inhabit. And Pearson likes it that way. "I've been trying to work with regionalism and appropriateness," he says. The visible ranch activity and open hills are important components of his design.

The process of designing a workspace for himself, his wife, and their children has been a true "live-work" project. Says designer Rain Turrell, "This house really came out of cocktail napkins, drawings on scrap wood, and yellow trace paper, which architects call 'bum wad.' It's the epitome of 'design-build.' It makes it a little more difficult for the builder when there's an evolution of the project. But it's been so successful in the end."

And according to Pearson, it's still an ongoing process. "Finishing for an architect never happens," he says. "It's evolutionary."

"I put together a distillation of a Western barn motif with west coast Eichler influences. That was my thinking on the evolution of what was the New Utopia."

"The house really glows at night," says interior designer Rain Turrell. "It has a wonderful ambience."

resources

BUILDERS, ARCHITECTS & DESIGNERS

Bridger Engineers, Inc.
2150 Analysis Drive
Bozeman, MT 59718
406.585.0590
www.bridgerengineers.com

Comma-Q Architecture, Inc.
Douglas J. Minarik, AIA,
  LEED AP
109 North Rouse Ave., #1
Bozeman, MT 59715
406.585.1112
dminarik@hotmail.com
www.commaq.com

Jonathan Foote, Architect & Planner
T Square Ranch
252 Convict Grade Road
Livingston, MT 59047
406.223.7899
job@tsquareranch.com

Goff Architecture Ltd.
Graham Goff, Architect
201 South Wallace Street,
  Suite A3
Bozeman, MT 59715
406.582.5845
www.goffarch.com

Halcyon House Interior Design
P.O. Box 68
Old Chelsea Station
New York, NY 10113
212.477.1941

Hilary Heminway Interiors
140 Briar Patch Road
Stonington, CT 06378
860.535.3110

JLF & Associates, Inc.
140 East Main Street
Bozeman, MT 59715
406.587.8888
www.jlfarchitects.com

Montana Mobile Cabins
Dawndi and Kipp Keim
P.O. Box 826
Whitehall, MT 59759
406.287.5030
www.montanamobilecabins.com

On Site Management
417 West Mendenhall Street
Bozeman, MT 59715
406.586.1500

Pearson Design Group
777 E. Main Street, Suite 203
Bozeman, MT 59715
406.587.1997
www.pearsondesigngroup.com

Polsky Architects
Tyler Shelton
469B Magnolia Avenue
Larkspur, CA 94939
415.927.1156
www.polskyarchitects.com

PRW Interiors
Patsy Psaledakis
303.881.2527

Rossi Scott
Designer
San Francisco, CA
rossione@pacbell.net

Dave Strike Custom Building
P.O. Box 712
Cody, WY 82414
307.587.6334

Studio Ryker
Lori Ryker, Architect
P.O. Box 838
Livingston, MT 59047
406.220.1099
www.studioryker.com

Sweet Grass Homesteads
Tom Norquist
Big Timber, MT
406.932.4243
homesteads@sweetgrass
  homesteads.com
Reclaimed log work

WESTERN FURNISHINGS, FURNITURE MAKERS & ARTISANS, SHOPS & GALLERIES

Britt Studios
Amber Britt
www.brittstudio.com
Handmade ceramic tiles

Building Materials Thrift Store
3990 Woodside Boulevard
Hailey, ID 83333
208.788.0014
*Reusable construction materials;
all proceeds benefit the Wood
River Land Trust*

Covert Workshops
Jim & Lynda Covert
2007 Public Street
Cody, WY 82414
lyndabcovert@gmail.com

Glass Roots of Montana
5920 Sourdough Road
Bozeman, MT 59715
406.579.5294
www.glassrootsofmontana.com
Custom recycled glass tile

Audrey Hall Photography
1106 West Park, #121
Livingston, MT 59047
406.222.2450
www.audreyhall.com

How Kola
1627 23rd Street
Cody, WY 82414
307.587.9814
Western furniture and accessories

John Tate Workroom
2308 North 7th Avenue
Bozeman, MT 59715
406.587.7463
www.johntateworkroom.com
Custom curtains, pillows, and draperies

Montana Expressions
2504 West Main Street
Bozeman, MT 59715
406.585.5839
www.montanaexpressions.com

Mimi London
Pacific Design Center
8687 Melrose Avenue,
  Suite G-168
Los Angeles, CA 90069
310.855.2567
www.mimilondon.com
High-end log furniture

Santos Furniture
P.O. Box 176
Cody, WY 82414
888.WOOD-GUY
www.lestersantos.com

Wood River Rustics
Ketchum, ID
208.726.1442

Vintage Lighting
www.vintagelighting.com
Antique lighting fixtures and lamps, both electric and gas

ART RESOURCES

Big Horn Gallery
1167 Sheridan Avenue
Cody, WY 82414
307.527.7587
www.bighorngalleries.com

Chaparral Fine Art
24 West Main Street
Bozeman, MT 59715
406.585.0029
www.chaparralfineart.com

Danforth Gallery
106 North Main Street
Livingston, MT 59047
406.222.6510

Legacy Gallery
7178 Main Street
Scottsdale, AZ 85251
480.945.1113
www.legacygallery.com

Thomas Nygard
135 East Main Street
Bozeman, MT 59715
406.586.3636
www.nygardgallery.com
Nineteenth- and twentieth-century American art

Simpson Gallagher Gallery
1161 Sheridan Avenue
Cody, WY 82414
307.587.4022
www.simpsongallagher
  gallery.com

Betsy Swartz Fine Art
Consulting
Bozeman, MT
406.585.8339
www.betsyswartzfineart.com

Visions West Gallery
34 West Main Street
Bozeman, MT 59715
406.522.9946
www.visionswestgallery.com

RANCH HOMES
DESIGN RESOURCES
Architects across the country adapted the suburban ranch house idea during the 1930s, 1940s, 1950s, and 1960s. Ranch house resources include:

Cliff May Registry
www.cliffmayregistry.com;
Registry of homes designed by ranch house architect Cliff May.

Lotta Living
www.lottaliving.com
Mid-century modern design resources.

Home Plans
www.homeplans.com
House plans, blueprints, home design, and homebuilding resources.

RESOURCES FOR
BUILDING IN THE WEST

The Sweet Grass Code of
the West
For a free copy, write to:
P.O. Box 71
Big Timber, MT 59011

WESTERN DESIGN
VENUES

Cody High Style
www.codyhighstyle.org
Juried furniture and fashion show held annually in September in Cody, Wyoming

Western Design
Conference
www.westerndesign
  conference.com
Juried exhibition of museum-quality functional art, held annually in September in Jackson, Wyoming